THE STORY OF THE
Lost Star

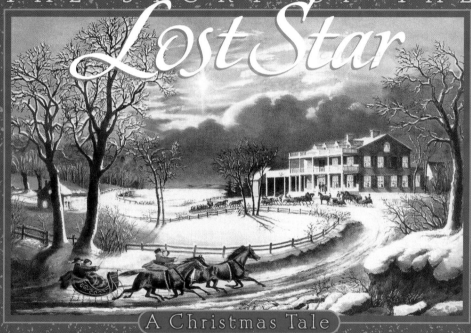

A Christmas Tale

Grace Livingston Hill

EW mm vrw Rtte NS

The Story of the Lost Star

Text copyright ©1932 by Grace Livingston Hill
Published by Harvest House Publishers
Eugene, Oregon 97402

Library of Congress Cataloging-in-Publication Data

Hill, Grace Livingston, 1865–1947.
    The story of the lost star / Grace Livingston Hill.
        p. cm.
    ISBN 0-7369-0371-2
    I. Title

    PS3515.I486 S693 2000
    813'.52—dc21

                                                        00-025904

Currier and Ives images on pages 4, 5, 9, 10, 11, 17, 18, 22, 26, 30, 34, 38, copyright © The
Museum of the City of New York, the Harry T. Peters Collection. Images published
between 1846 and 1868. Used with permission.

Design and Production by Koechel Peterson and Associates, Minneapolis, Minnesota

Scripture quotations are from the King James Version.

Printed in Hong Kong

00 01 02 03 04 05 06 07 08 09 / IM / 10 9 8 7 6 5 4 3 2

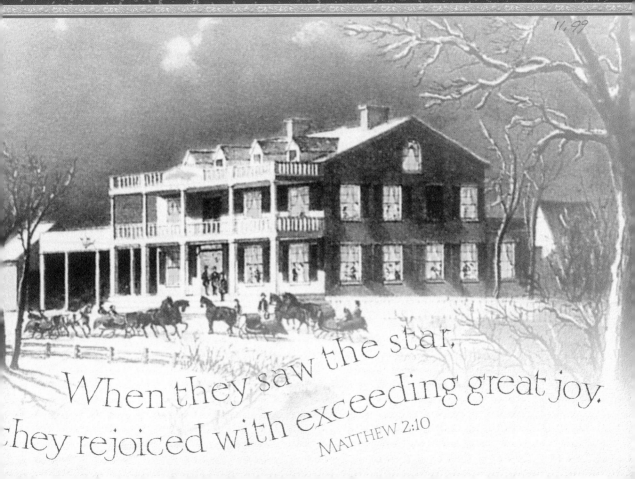

When they saw the star,
they rejoiced with exceeding great joy.

MATTHEW 2:10

 bout a week before Christmas in a small city of the East there

appeared in the Lost and Found column this advertisement:

Lost: Sometime between the
World War and the present morning,
The Star of Bethlehem. The finder
will confer everlasting favor and
receive a reward of ten thousand
dollars if returned to the owner
between the hours of sundown and
midnight on Christmas Eve.

(SIGNED) GEORGE K. HAMILTON,
Eleven, Harvard Place

The typesetter blinked and paused in his busy work, read it again and wondered. Ten thousand dollars! Was it a joke? It must be a mistake! But no, it was paid for. It must go in. He punched away at his machine and the lines appeared in the type, but his thoughts were busy. Ten thousand dollars! With that he could, with self-respect, marry Mary! He would not have been John if he had not thought of that first.

Star of Bethlehem

eorge K. Hamilton. That was the rich guy who lived in the big house, with one blind wall stuck on its side that everybody said was a picture gallery. He was rolling in wealth so it must be real. But what was this thing he had lost that was worth everlasting favor and ten thousand dollars? A jewel? A silver tablet? Something of intrinsic historic value perhaps?

Something that must be well known, or the writer would not have spoken of it in that off-hand indefinite way as *the* Star of Bethlehem, as if there were but one. Bethlehem – Bethlehem – that was the place where they made steel! Steel! Why – steel of course.

eorge K. Hamilton. Hamilton the steel king! Ah! Why hadn't he thought of it at once?

And why couldn't he go to Bethlehem and find out all about it? He was the first one, excepting the editor of the Lost and Found column, to see this ad. Why wouldn't he stand first chance of the reward if he worked it right?

To be sure, there was a possibility that someone, who knew just what this star was, would be able to get on its track sooner. But if he caught the first train in the morning he would have a good start before anyone read the morning papers.

H e would be through with his work by three A.M. at the latest, and there was a train at five. He would have time to get back to his boarding place and clean up a bit, perhaps scribble a note to Mary telling her to be ready for the wedding.

—eleven—

is fingers flew over the keys of his machine as he laid his plans, and his heart throbbed with excitement over the great opportunity that had flung its open door right in his humble path. Ten thousand dollars!

Early dawn saw him dressed in his best and hurrying on his way to Bethlehem amid a train load of laborers going out for the day's work. But he saw not pick nor shovel nor dinner pail, nor noted greasy overalls and sleepy-eyed companions. Before his shining eyes was a star, sometimes silver, sumptuously engraved, sometimes gold and set in sparkling jewels, leading him on into the day of adventure.

He essayed to question his fellow seatmate about that star:

"You live in Bethlehem? Did you ever see the Star of Bethlehem?"

But the man shook his head dumbly:

"Me no spak L'angla!"

Arriving in the City of Steel he went straight to the news agent:

"Have you been here some time?"

"Born here."

"Then tell me, have you a Star of Bethlehem?"

"Did you ever see the Star of Bethlehem?"

he agent shook his head.

"Don't smoke that kind. Don't keep that kind. Try the little cigar store down the street." He swung himself under the shelf and, shouldering a pile of morning papers, rushed off down the platform.

Out in the street John stopped a man whose foot was just mounting the running board of his car:

"Do you know anything about the Star of Bethlehem?"

ever heard of it, Man. A Ford's good enough for me!"

He swung into his car and shot away from the curb hurriedly.

He asked a little girl who was hurrying away from the bakery with a basket of bread.

"Why, Star-of-Bethlehem is a flower," she said, "a little green and white starry flower with pointed petals. It grows in the meadow over there in the summertime, but it's all gone now. You can't find Stars-of-Bethlehem this time of year!" And she stared after him for a silly fool.

He asked a passer on the street:

"Can you tell me how to find out about the Star of Bethlehem?"

"Can you help me find the Star of Bethlehem?"

he man tapped him lightly on the shoulder with a wink and advised him knowingly, with a thumb pointing down a side alley:

"You better not mention that openly, brother. There's been several raids around here lately and the police are wise. It ain't safe."

About this time the Bishop back at home was opening the morning paper at the breakfast table as he toyed with his grapefruit and coffee:

"Ha, ha!" he said as his eye traveled down the column idly and paused at the Lost and Found, "Listen to this, Bella. Poor old George has got 'em again. He probably thinks he is going to die this time.

’ll just step in and have a little talk on theology with him this morning and set his mind at rest. No need for that ten thousand dollars to go out of the church. We might as well have it as some home for the Feeble Minded."

Bella left her coffee and came around to read the advertisement, her face lighting intelligently:

"Oh, Basil! Do you think you can work it?" she cried delightedly.

"Why, sure. He's just a little daffy on religion now because he's been sick. The last time I saw him he asked me how we could know any of the creeds were true when they were all so different. I'll smooth it all out for him, and make him give another ten thousand or so to the Social Service work of our church, and he'll come across handsomely, you'll see. I'd better go at once. It won't do to wait, there are too many kinds of crooks on the lookout for just such a soft ten thousand as this." And he took his hat and coat and hurried out.

The Professor at his meagre breakfast table, worrying about his sick wife, and how he cold afford to keep his eldest son in college, happened on the item.

He set down his coffee cup untasted and stepped to his bookshelves taking down several wise treatises on astronomy.

**A** sweet faced saint in an invalid chair read and pondered and murmured thoughtfully: "Poor soul! What's happened to the man's Bible?"

Before night the one little shop in the city that made a speciality of astronomical instruments had been drained of everything in the shape of a searcher of the heavens, and a rush order had gone on to New York by telegraph for more telescopes of various sizes and prices, while a boy in the back office who was good at lettering was busy making a copy of the advertisement to fasten up in the plate glass window, with special electric lights playing about it and a note below:

"Come in and order your telescope now before they are all gone, and get into line for the great sky prize! We have 'em! All prices!"

Far into the evening the crowd continued around that window and many who had glasses at home hurried away to search for them, building air castles of how they would spend the ten thousand dollars when they got it.

Even before the day was half over the office of the University was besieged by eager visitors come to question wise ones, a folded newspaper furtively held under each applicant's arm.

s evening drew on, shadowy figures stole forth to high places and might have been seen scanning the heavens, and now and then consulting a book by means of a pocket flashlight. More than one young student worked into the small hours of the night with reference books scattered about him, writing a many-paged treatise on Star of Stars, some to prove that the star was a myth, and others that it was still in existence and would one day appear again as bright as of old. Even the police, coming suddenly upon lurking stargazers far toward morning, began to question what had taken hold of the town.

oming home on the late train from a fruitless search for an unknown quantity which was not there, John Powers sat wearily back in the fusty seat of the common car and took out the worn advertisement from his pocket to read it once more.

The lost Star of Bethlehem! What could it be? He had searched the steel city from end to end without finding so much as a trace of tradition or story about a star in connection with that town.

He had met with more rebuffs and strange suggestions than ever before in his life together, and he was dog-weary and utterly discouraged. If only he had not written that hopeful letter to Mary in the morning!

Now perhaps she would already be planning to have the wedding soon, and where was the money coming from to provide the little home?

Of course it just might happen that the star had been lost up in the city after all. Why else should the advertisement have been put in the city paper and not in the Bethlehem local? But even so he had hoped great things from this trip to Bethlehem and now he had only wasted a day and car fare, and had gotten nowhere at all.

At a local station a loud-mouthed traveler got off, leaving his recent seatmate without anyone to talk to, and presently he joined John Powers and entered into conversation, being one of those men who is never happy unless his tongue is wagging. In the course of their talk, John found himself asking the old question again:

"You say you are from Bethlehem? Did you ever hear of a star in connection with that town? Was there any memorial tablet or monument or emblem or anything in the shape of a star that has been stolen away? Star of Bethlehem it was called, do you know anything about it?"

The stranger stared blankly and shook his head:

ounds to me as if it might be a song, or book mebbe. If you knowed who wrote it you might find out at one o' the schools. My Johnny says you can find out almost anything if you know who wrote it. Ever been a Mason? Might be some kind of a Masonic badge, mightn't it?"

The man got out at the next station and Powers leaned back wearily and thought how he had failed. His mind seemed too tired to think any longer on the subject.

An old lady in a queer bonnet with many bundles at her feet and a basket beside her out of which stuck a pair of turkey's feet, leaned over suddenly and touched him on the shoulder:

"Laddie, hae ye tried the auld Buik?" she asked timidly. "I'm thinkin' ye'll find it all there."

"I beg your pardon!" said Powers, lifting his hat courteously and thinking how the blue of her eyes had a light like that in Mary's eyes.

He arose from his seat and went back to sit beside her. Then somehow the blue of her eyes made him unafraid, and he told her all about the ten thousand dollars and his fruitless trip to Bethlehem.

h, but laddie, ye're on the wrong track entirely," said the old lady. "The Star o' Bethlehem's in the auld Buik. I ken it's no the fashion to read it these days, but the worruld lost sight of a lot besides the things it wanted to forget when it set out to put its Bibles awa! Hunt up yer Mither's Bible, lad, and study it out. The star arose in the East ye ken, and the folks who saw it first was those that was lookin' fer its arisin'. The star's *na* lost. It led to the little King ye ken, an' it'll always lead to the King if a body seeks with all the heirt, fer that is the promise: 'An' ye shall find me, when ye shall seek fer Me with all yer heirts.'

"May like the puir buddy who wrote the bit lines in the paper was longin' fer the King hisself an' wanted the star to guide him, but ye ken ye can't purchase the gifts of God wi' silver ner gold. The mon may lay his ten thousand baubles at the fut of the throne, but he'll find he must go his own self across the desert, and wait mayhap, before he'll ever see the shinin' of the Star. But you'll not turn back yerself now you've started, laddie! Go find the King fer yerself. Look in the Gospels an' read the story. It's passin' wonderful an' lovely. This is my station now, and I'll be leavin' ye, but it'll be a glad Christmas time fer you ef you find the little King, an' *ye'll find Him* sure, if ye seek on with all yer heirt."

he doorway to the fine old Hamilton mansion on Harvard Place was besieged from morning to night all that week by aspirants wishing to speak with the Master, but to all the brave and dignified servitor who answered the door replied:

"My master is away. He cannot speak with you until the time appointed. If any then have found the lost treasure they may come and claim the reward. But they must come bringing it with them. None others need present themselves."

Even the Bishop had not been able to gain admittance. He was much annoyed about it. He was afraid others would get ahead of him. He had written a letter, but he knew it had not yet been opened for the last time he called he had seen it lying on the console in the hall with a lot of other unopened letters. The Bishop was very certain that if he could have audience *first,* all would be well. He was sure he could explain the philosophy of life and the mystery of the star quite satisfactorily and soothingly.

 efore John Powers had gone back to work that night of his return from Bethlehem, he had gone to the bottom of an old chest and hunted out his mother's Bible. It was worn and dropping apart in places, but he put it tenderly on his bed, and following an impulse, dropped to his knees beside it, laying his lips against its dusty covers. Somehow the very look of the old worn covers brought back his childhood days and a sense of sin in that he had wandered so far from the path in which his mother had set his young feet.

All that week he gave all the extra time he had to studying about the star. He did not even go to see Mary.

He lost sight of the ten thousand dollars in his interest in the star itself. He was now seeking to find that star for himself, not for the reward that had been offered. He wanted to find the King who was also a Saviour.

The last night before it came time for him to go to his work, he dropped upon his knees once more beside the little tattered book, and prayed:

"Oh Jesus Christ, Saviour of the world, I thank Thee that Thou has sent Thy star to guide me to Thee. I worship Thee, and I give myself to Thee forever."

On Christmas Eve, when the door of the mansion was thrown open, a large throng of people entered, They were speedily admitted, one by one, to audience with the master of the house, until, in an incredibly short space of time, the waiting room was emptied of philosophers and dreamers and ambitious ones. Even the Bishop had been courteously sent his way. Only three were left, three wise ones, and two of them were women!

ne was an old woman with a burr upon her tongue and a Bible in her hand; one was a young girl with blue starry eyes and a bit of a Testament in the folds of her gown where she kept her fingers between the leaves to a place. The third was John Powers, standing within the shadow of a heavy curtain beside a deepset window looking out at the great shining of a bright star, with peace upon his face. He turned about as the door closed after the Bishop and glanced at the two women. The girl looked up and their eyes met.

"Mary!"

"John!"

There was scarcely time to recognize the old woman before the door opened and George K. Hamilton, keen of eye, sharp of feature, eager of expression, walked in and looked from one to the other searching each face questioningly.

The young man stepped forward to meet him and Mary saw for the first time that a worn little Bible was in his hand.

John spoke in such a ringing voice of certainty:

"Sir, I want to tell you first that I have not come for your money. When I began this search it was in hope of the reward, but I've found the Star itself, and it led me to the King, and now I've brought it to you because I want you to have it too. You'll find it in this Book. It has to be searched for, but it's there. And when you have found it I've been thinking you'll maybe want to sell all that you have and give to the poor and go and follow *Him*. But I am not one of those poor any longer, for I *have found the King*! Come, Mary, shall we go?"

Then up rose the old Scotch woman from her place near the door:

"I've just one more word to say, an' ye'll find it in yon Buik: 'Arise, shine; for thy light is come, and the Glory of the Lord is risen upon thee.' That star isn't lost, sir, an' never was! Never will be! It's up in the

A single star
shone softly through the
Christmas night.

heavens waiting till the King has need of it again, and some day it will burst upon the world again and they will all know that it has been there all the time!"

The Master was left alone in his mansion with the book in his hand and a strange, awed feeling of the Presence of God in his room.

He looked wonderingly, doubtfully, down at the book, and then wistfully out through his richly draped window to where a single star shone softly through the Christmas night.

For we have seen his star in the east, and are come to worship him . . .

MATTHEW 2:2